YellowStones

What do you see?

Caroline McClure

I see a Canada goose soaring in the blue.

What do you see?

I see a bison snorting at you.

What do you see?

I see a boot with a hiker's missing sock.

What do you see?

I SEE A GROUSE NESTING IN THE ROCKS.

What do you see?

I SEE ELK ANTLERS, MAJESTIC AND WIDE.

What do you see?

I SEE A HORSE
ON A DUSTY TRAIL RIDE.

What do you see?

I SEE A PAINT POT
SO BUBBLY AND PINK.

What do you see?

Oh my, what is that stink?

What do you see?

I SEE A FROG GETTING READY TO LEAP.

What do you see?

I see curly horns on a bighorn sheep.

What do you see?

I see a coyote, keen and sly.

What do you see?

I see a bison skull, how did it die?

What do you see?

I SEE A BUTTERFLY FLITTING OVERHEAD.

What do you see?

I SEE AN ANGLER IN A STREAM BED.

What do you see?

I SEE A CANOE ON THE WATER BRIGHT.

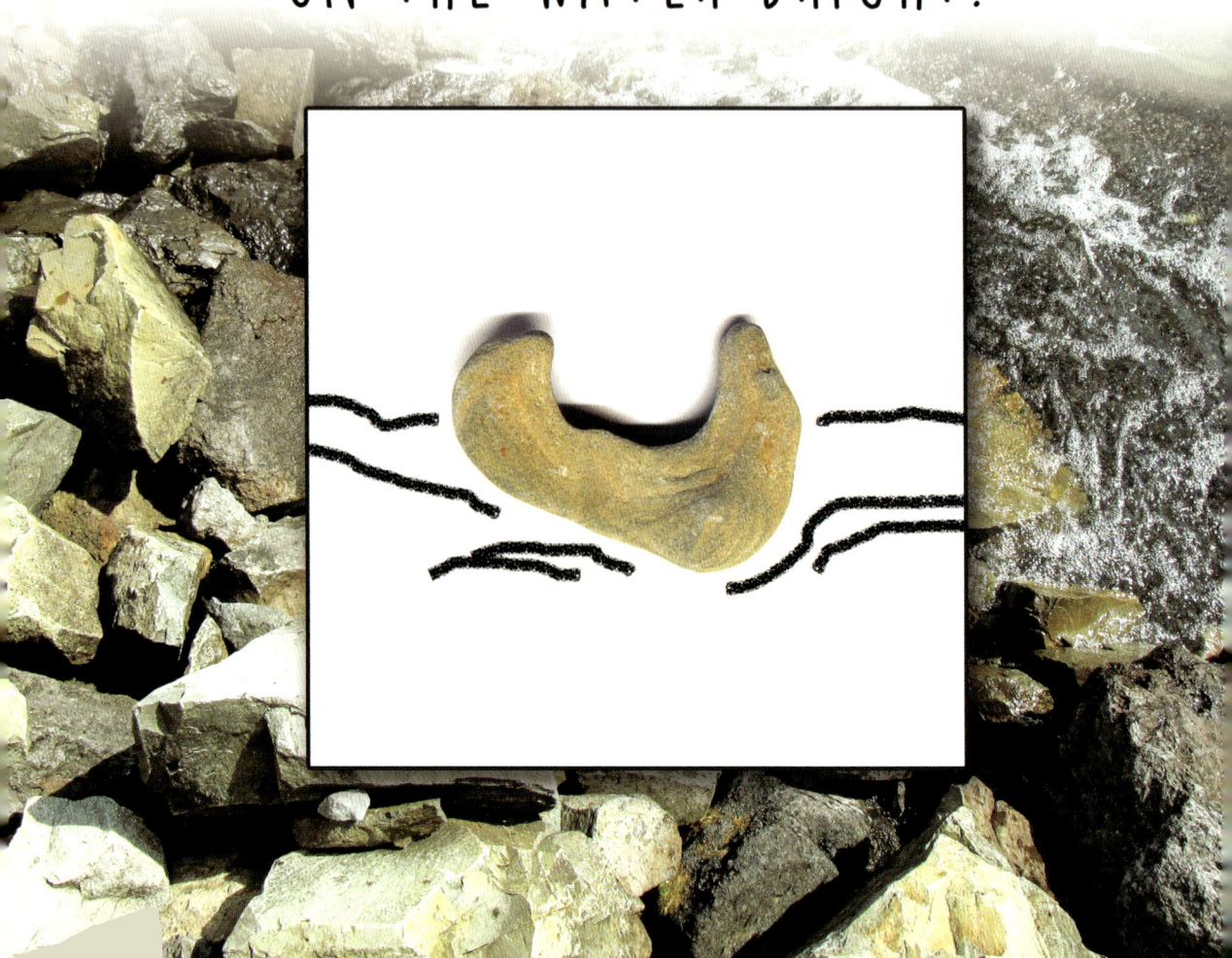

What do you see?

I see an owl, creature of the night.

What do you see?

I SEE A BEAR CUB LOOKING FOR HIS MOTHER.

What do you see?

I SEE A FOX KIT HIDING FROM HER BROTHER.

What do you see?

I SEE THE TAIL OF
A GLIDING GRAY JAY.

What do you see?

I see Lower Falls, can you feel the spray?

What do you see?

I SEE A FISH DARTING IN A SHALLOW POOL.

What do you see?

I SEE A MOOSE SLURPING
A DRINK SO COOL.

What do you see?

I SEE A MARMOT, CURIOUS CREATURE.

What do you see?

I see Old Faithful, Yellowstone's most famous feature.

ISBN: 978-1-59152-214-0 • © 2018 by Caroline McClure

All rights reserved. This book may not be reproduced in whole or in part by any means (with the exception of short quotes for the purpose of review) without the permission of the publisher.

For more information or to order extra copies of this book call Farcountry Press toll free at (800) 821-3874.

Produced by Sweetgrass Books, PO Box 5630, Helena, MT 59604; (800) 821-3874; www.sweetgrassbooks.com • Produced and printed in the United States of America. • 21 20 19 18   1 2 3 4